GOD BECAME MAN

GOD BECAME MAN

By: Bishop Poemen

God Became Man

ST SHENOUDA MONASTERY
8419 Putty Rd,
Putty, NSW, 2330
Sydney, Australia

www.stshenoudamonastery.org.au

ISBN 13: 978-0-9941910-0-7

Cover Design:

Hani Ghaly
Begoury Graphics
www.Go2printOnline.toprint.com.au

Contents

About the Author

HG Bishop Poemen (formerly Kamal Habeeb) was a teacher by profession, having graduated with a Master's degree in Education and Psychology. He worked as a high school teacher for many years. In 1964 he decided to resign from his job and dedicate his life to Christ wherein he went to live at a consecrated house, along with other men who dedicated their life to Christ, in Helwaan (Beet El-Takrees) under the leadership of Fr. Matthew the poor (Matta El-Maskeen).

Shortly after the ordination of Pope Shenouda III to the throne of the see of St. Mark in 1971, Kamal Habeeb went to follow the monastic path. Shortly thereafter His Holiness ordained him as a Bishop to the city of Malawi. In September 1981, he was among the clergy who were imprisoned and was counted among those who became worthy to suffer for His Name.

HG Bishop Poemen served the region of Malawi with diligence in which he founded a Theological College which was badly needed in that region of Upper Egypt. HG Bishop Poemen has written over 21 books, 20 Booklets, many Pamphlets, and he wrote a regular column in El-Keraazah, the official Coptic Church Weekly Magazine. His books covered: Christian Education, Celibacy, Love, Worship, Rural Evangelism, Teenage, The Body and Sex, Christian Vision of Evangelical work, Liturgy, Christian Family, Contemplation, Spiritual Fasting, and a program for High School Christian Education.

Introduction

In the Old Testament, feasts were not an excuse for holidays, or to find time for relaxation, but the feast was a remembrance of the promises God made with His people and the renewal of the people's commitment with Jehovah the God of Israel.

In the New Testament, Jesus bestowed dignity on feasts, its meaning and glory. The Lord attended all the feasts while He was on earth in the flesh. He contributed and celebrated with the people in the Temple with the feasts of Passover, Tabernacles, Dedication, etc.

However, He was very cautious not to let the symbol overshadow the symbolised, and to transfer the mind from the shadow to the truth itself. We will give some examples from the Gospel of Saint John:

In chapter two it is written: "Now the Passover of the Jews was at hand, and Jesus went up to Jerusalem. And He found in the temple those who sold oxen and sheep and doves, and the money changers doing business...He drove them all out of the temple... So the Jews answered and said to Him, "What sign do You show to us, since

You do these things?" Jesus answered and said to them, "Destroy this temple, and in three days I will raise it up" (John 2:13-19). Referring to His body is the real Passover, the real temple!

In chapter five "After this there was a feast of the Jews, and Jesus went up to Jerusalem. Now there is in Jerusalem by the Sheep Gate a pool, which is called in Hebrew, Bethesda, having five porches" (John 5:1-2). No angel or lamb was able to save the paralysed man, but Jesus the Lamb of God who carries the sins of the world, who is capable of clearing man from sin, sends him off carrying his bed victoriously.

It was a Sabbath, but Jesus healed on the Sabbath, because it was He who restored to humanity the real meaning of the Sabbath "The Sabbath was made for man, and not man for the Sabbath" (Mark 2:26).

In chapter six, "Now the Passover, a feast of the Jews, was near" (John 6:4). the following verses (5-14) explain to us how the Lord fed the multitudes with five loaves and two fish. He then goes on to talk about Himself as the real heavenly Passover "Most assuredly, I say to you, Moses did not give you the bread from heaven, but My Father gives you the true bread from heaven" (John 6:32) and "I am the bread of life. He who comes to Me shall never hunger, and he who believes in Me shall never thirst. But I said to you that you have seen Me and yet do not believe. All that the Father gives Me will come to Me, and the one who comes to Me I will by no means cast out. For I have come down from heaven, not to do My own will, but the will of Him who sent Me. This is the will of the Father who sent Me, that of all He has given Me I should lose nothing, but should raise it up at the last day. And this is the will of Him who sent Me, that everyone who sees the Son and believes in Him may have everlasting life; and I will raise him up at the last day" (John 6:35-40).

In chapter seven, "Now the Jews' Feast of Tabernacles was at hand... Now about the middle of the feast Jesus went up into the temple and taught. And the Jews marveled...On the last day, that great day of the feast, Jesus stood and cried out, saying, "If anyone thirsts, let him come to Me and drink. He who believes in Me, as the Scripture has said, out of his heart will flow rivers of living water." But this He spoke concerning the Spirit, whom those believing in Him would receive" (John 7:2-40). Such did the water flow on the steps of the Temple and the Levites poured the water on the steps as a remembrance of the water that exploded out of the rock. However Jesus spoke about the living water and the Spirit from which flows spiritual rivers in the hearts of believers.

In chapter twelve, six days before the Passover, Jesus came to Bethany and Mary took a pound of very costly oil of spikenard and anointed the feet of Jesus. When Judas Iscariot was annoyed by what she had done, Jesus said "Let her alone; she has kept this for the day of My burial" (John 12:7). And so was the death of Jesus, the real Passover and the true crossover for all the believers from darkness to light and from death to life.

Likewise, throughout the Gospel we find that our teacher John is very careful to bring out the real spiritual meaning of the feast in the person of our Lord Jesus Christ.

Before Christ, the feast was a symbol that leads the way for His coming. After the Incarnation and His entrance into time; the feast became a renewal and a remembrance for His blessed Person.

We have placed our articles and contemplations regarding feasts in this perspective, and most of these studies were published in the El-Keraza magazine during the last five years. We have collected them in two volumes for every reader, deacon and preacher, to keep and to serve them for many liturgical years to come.

May God bless this effort and every effort that works for the Glory of His Holy name, Amen.

With the grace of God

Bishop Poemen (Bishop of Malawy)

Chapter 1

With the Newborn of Bethlehem

In Christianity, knowing God is not just in theory. Even the devil believes and fears, but is not saved. Truly knowing God is by experience where the Lord Christ is to every believer; God, the Messiah, the Saviour, the Shepherd, the Bread of life, the focus of his/her life.

It is Christ the Saviour

This is the first experience in our encounter with the Lord; He was born in Bethlehem in order to give us the second birth through water and the Spirit.

In baptism, the old is buried and everything becomes new. In this holy sacrament we receive salvation from Christ. He gives us the new man and dresses us with a wedding gown and we become children of God, those who were born, not of blood, nor of the will of the flesh, nor of the will of man, but of God.

When the prodigal son left for a distant country delighting in the futilities of the world, the Lord Jesus, the Saviour, had His bosom open awaiting the return of the son with eagerness and kindness. The soul remains far from the green pastures to which the good shepherd guides it to rest, and so, the soul hungers and thirsts and the person finds himself in a void and isolation and in need of returning to the Saviour. Jesus the Saviour comes knocking on the door so that the soul awakens from its loss and sleep hence the only thing it can do is shout "have mercy".

Say a single word: O Master help me so that I can begin. Glance at me O Saviour to strengthen me and I may rise. Grant me a touch my God that I may get up and hasten to return.

As the eye is filled with warm tears and the heart with sadness over the days eaten by locusts, the soul propels with joy because it is going through the repentance phase and the renewal of the covenant of salvation.

"And she will bring forth a Son, and you shall call His name Jesus, for He will save His people from their sins" (Matthew 1:21). In this, the spirit hears the sound of its saviour saying "Awake, awake, put on strength, O arm of the Lord! Awake as in the ancient days, In the generations of old. Are You not the arm that cut Rahab apart, And wounded the serpent? Are You not the One who dried up the sea, The waters of the great deep; That made the depths of the sea a road For the redeemed to cross over? So the ransomed of the Lord shall return, And come to Zion with singing, With everlasting joy on their heads. They shall obtain joy and gladness; Sorrow and sighing shall flee away. "I, even I, am He who comforts you" (Isaiah 51:9-12).

Rise O spirit and be enlightened, because your Light has come and the Lord's glory has shone over you. It is an encounter which does great work in the life of the believer.

• Simon left everything after his encounter with the calling of love.

• Saul became dedicated to the service of the Word after his encounter with the Saviour.

• Moses the black became a monk and left the world after he learned the way, the truth and the life.

Every person whose heart has been entered by Jesus the Saviour and has had a real encounter is able to say with John the beloved "that which we have seen and heard we declare to you, that you also may have fellowship with us" (1 John 1-3).

Emmanuel our God is with us

The spirit that passes through the first encounter enters into the second encounter by grace, in which the Lord guides the spirit like a good shepherd and an experienced pastor. In this encounter, the spirit sings with David the prophet "The Lord is my shepherd; I shall not want. He makes me to lie down in green pastures; He leads me beside the still waters... Your rod and Your staff, they comfort me" (Psalm 22:1-4).

The good shepherd strikes the ground with His rod so that His sheep hear His sound and follow Him. The loving Father holds His staff and is ready to discipline every spirit that wishes to deviate from the path.

Emmanuel, which means God is with us, raises His rod and disperses all His enemies from His face and the wolves that are lurking, awaiting to devour someone, escape.

He warns and rebukes every soul that began to walk with Him, but desired to delight in the midst of the twisted paths, to become occupied by distant and broken wells where the merciless enemy dwells.

God is with us is a song of joy repeated by those treading the path as a song of victory, praising with it the lion coming from the tribe of Judah and they see and encounter in His company growth in grace, wisdom and spiritual stature.

Let us be complete as one

Christianity did not stop at the first two encounters. It first gives forgiveness of sins to every confessing sinner and in the second encounter it provides attention to every spirit that submits and is eager for eternal life, but it goes further to give an encounter with the life of unity with the real vine.

Christ our God through His incarnation gave us what is His (let us praise Him and glorify Him and exalt Him above all) and the Word became flesh in order to grant us a life of unity with Him and His good Father in goodness and eternal joy.

The Apostle Peter sees that the aim of Christianity is to be united in God's nature and the unity for us believers is with the Father and His son Jesus Christ - just as written in John 17.

The Lord wanted to clarify to us this encounter, so He resembled Himself as the vine and honoured us by making us the branches of the vine. Every branch that bears fruit, He purifies in order for it to bear more fruit. No branch can bear fruit on its own if it was not fastened to the vine. So it is with us if we are not fastened to Him.

In the Lord's last intercessory prayer He revealed to us the purpose of His incarnation, birth and salvation when He said "Holy Father, keep through Your name those whom You have given Me, that they may be one as We are" (John 17:11).

These are three simple encounters with the newborn of the manger. In the beginning we encounter the Saviour because Jesus saves us from our sins. We tread behind Him in the path for He is Emmanuel, God is with us, and shepherds us with His staff and rod.

In the depth of life with Him, we are granted a life of unity with the Father and His Son so that we are "complete as one"

'O beloved' is the voice of the Lord to us.

To encounter Him in repentance as Jesus the saviour.

To submit to Him as Emmanuel, God is with us. Let Him take control of our spirit, to keep us in spiritual perseverance.

We stand fast and unite with Him in the sacrament of the Eucharist, the sacrament of the true vine.

Chapter 2

What Does God's Incarnation Mean

In the past God communicated with man in many ways. We see Him appearing in the form of a flame of fire in the burning bush and in other times in the form of an Angel and also as a pillar of fire. However, for the Son of God to become incarnate and human like us to resemble us in everything except sin is a matter that exceeds every imagination, logic and human intellect. If God's incarnation is the greatest and most important event in the history of humanity, then what does it mean for God and man?

Incarnation is a revealing of the essence of love

If the aim of man's creation is for this unique creature to enjoy a life of sacred unity with God, then the incarnation can also be understood from the perspective of love. For just as God loved man and created him to enjoy life and have happiness; He gave him His love, His glory. God came to him and took his form and was incarnate in order to restore to him the life of sacred unity. Thus God became man in order to revive us from our fall and raise us from our death and grant us eternal life after death, which we justly deserved due to Adam's (our first father) disobedience.

On this, the Holy Gospel says "For God so loved the world that He gave His only begotten Son, that whoever believes in Him should not perish but have everlasting life" (John 3:16). It was the intention of the Father to satisfy the hunger of this creature, in which case He has provided him with the true living bread, and granted him through His incarnation the partaking of the living bread, which descended from heaven. Therefore, the Lord said with His pure mouth that whoever eats Me will live by Me (John 6:51-58).

If sin has torn the unity between God and man, then the Lord Christ has restored it through His incarnation and has abolished it into eternity. It is only through His person can man encounter God. Unity between divinity and humanity was unification without mingling, confusion or alteration. This is what the Apostle Paul voiced in his letter to Ephesians "just as He chose us in Him before the foundation of the world, that we should be holy and without blame before Him in love" (Ephesians 1:4). Likewise the Son said to the heavenly Father "And I have declared to them Your name, and will declare it, that the love with which You loved Me may be in them, and I in them" (John 17:26)

The heavenly Father's intention was that the Son would unite with man in his humanly nature to resemble His brothers in everything just like St. Paul the Apostle, the author of the book of Hebrews says "Therefore, in all things He had to be made like His brethren, that He might be a merciful and faithful High Priest in things pertaining to God, to make propitiation for the sins of the people" (Hebrews 2:17). Also he says "the children have partaken of flesh and blood, He Himself likewise shared in the same, that through death He might destroy him who had the power of death, that is, the devil, and release those who through fear of death were all their lifetime subject to bondage" (Hebrews 2:14-15).

From that we can confer that the love of the Holy Trinity is the perspective from which we can understand the doctrine of God's incarnation and it carries two completely different dimensions: The salvation from man's sin and secondly the unity of man in life with God. "that which we have seen and heard we declare to you, that you also may have fellowship with us; and truly our fellowship is with the Father and with His Son Jesus Christ" (1 John 1:3) "For as in Adam all die, even so in Christ all shall be made alive" (1 Corinthians 15:22).

The incarnation is the centre of human history

If it was not for the incarnation of the Son and His entrance into our human history and His desired abidance to our festivities, life would not have meaning. This being due to the fact that man is constantly under the sway of time, the burden of stress, boredom, weariness and despair. This is what a contemporary French Atheist philosopher expressed by saying: "I do not know a meaning for my life, my existence is a mistake there is no explanation for it." As for the Christian, he understands his purpose and understands the meaning of his life very well for the Lord Jesus became to us wisdom, righteousness, holiness and salvation from God.

Life after incarnation became a message and everyone who believes in the newborn of Bethlehem realises clearly that life is no longer eating, drinking and amusement followed by loss and death. God has entered the human history in order for the human to enter the depth of Gods' heart.

• Life after Christ has become for Christ. "For if we live, we live to the Lord; and if we die, we die to the Lord. Therefore, whether we live or die, we are the Lord's" (Romans 14:8).

• "He died for all, that those who live should live no longer for themselves, but for Him who died for them and rose" (2 Corinthians 5:15).

• What He has made alive in Christ now stands. "I live by faith in the Son of God, who loved me and gave Himself for me" (Galatians 2:20).

Seeing then from that perspective, there is no longer a "human problem" or a problem in life with all that is in it from good to bad, happiness and pain. Faith has an eye that sees matters which cannot be seen and believes that everything works together for the good of those who love God and believes that Emmanuel is with us and in the midst of us.

Incarnation has given a meaning to time for it is through the Incarnation that we understood the past through God's dispensation and the heavenly Father's plan in preparing humanity to welcome the newborn of

Bethlehem and this is what the Bible expressed in the saying "when the fullness of time had come" (Galatians 4:4). The fullness of time is the completion of the dispensations of the Old Testament.

It is the fulfillment of the caretakers' plan as described by Clement of Alexandria, who used historical events and Israel's law with all its Fathers, Judges, Kings, Priests and Children for the teaching and promotion of humanity and its preparation spiritually and academically in order to be able to accept the greatest gift given by the Father to humanity and that is His beloved Son in whom His heart was pleased. This acceptance came through the mouth of the ambassador of all of humanity, the pure virgin Saint Mary when she said "Behold the maidservant of the Lord! Let it be to me according to your word" (Luke 1:38)

The past was a preparation for the incarnation. The present is an enjoyment of the incarnation through the church and its godly sacraments. The future is the expectation of the second coming, fearful and full of glory when the chosen are completed, and God ends time when the members of the church are complete, which is the purpose of existence. A theologian spoke about this saying "The world was created for the purpose of becoming a church" for God's incarnation revealed to us that God worked in history "My Father has been working until now, and I have been working" (John 5:17). He worked in the past and continues to work now and will continue to work using all favourable and unfavourable time events, the stubborn and the submissive for the glorification of the Lord in His church with the glory which is His with the Father. We Christians believe that God works in us and in history for the realisation of His intentions.

Christians believe that God's incarnation did not cause change in His Holy essence. Whoever believes that God created man from soil from a specific place and in a certain point in time, believes also that just because God was incarnate in a certain point in time and in a confined space does not make Him confined and does not cause change or exchange.

The responsibility of the church towards the Holy Body

The movement (action) descending from heaven must be met by supporting action from man. God descended from His glory and united with us and became one of us, with us and within us. Therefore, His love must be met with passionate love from the hearts of His believers and lovers. St John the Apostle says, 'Behold what manner of love the Father has bestowed on us, that we should be called children of God! (1 John 3:1). And 'Beloved, if God so loved us, we also ought to love one another' (1 John 4:11).

If the Son has descended to us, it was so that He would transfer the human thought to His person and focus their senses onto Himself as St Athanasius the Apostle said in his book - On the Incarnation of the Word. This is exactly what St Paul expressed "For our citizenship is in heaven, from which we also eagerly wait for the Savior, the Lord Jesus Christ" (Philippians 3:20). In the second coming of our Lord Jesus full of glory, we will witness those who are saved, those whose hearts were occupied with the love of their saviour who descended to them to raise them to Him.

We will see martyrs who were beheaded by the sword and the heavens were opened for them to see the Son of God in His glory, to see the desire of their hearts and their life's hope.

We will see monks and hermits who denied themselves from humanity and humanistic things to keep their hands lifted up for prayer and their hearts kindled with love for the heavenly groom.

We will see servants; preachers, teachers and ordinary people who tired abundantly for His name and in their last breath uttered the same words of that which is in the last verse of revelations:

"Come O Lord Jesus, yes come quickly..."

Chapter 3

With the Wise Men in the East

The wise men looked towards heaven and their eyes were enlightened. The one who looks above entreats God's mercy and accepts His wisdom. God's wisdom surely comes from above, from the Father of lights and the one who fixes his eyes towards heaven and has faith and hope will not be ashamed.

What is to prevent us from looking with the wise men to see the star in the east? Or is it that we look to ourselves? The self is a prison and the perimeter surrounding it is death - David says 'Bring my soul out of prison' Psalm 142:7. We look at the faces of people and we see lust and anger. For this, Paul being inspired cautiously said that he determined not to know anything except Jesus Christ and Him crucified. The wise men were not believers, but were heathen. The Scribes and Pharisees were not only believers but were scholars and knowledgeable, however, the truth was revealed to others and denied from them. God bypasses all man's partialities and looks at the heart alone.

The opening of the internal eye enabling it to see the truth is heavenly knowledge and God's work. The fathers in their writings point to the sacrament of baptism as the sacrament of enlightenment. They say that praying especially with constantly teary eyes will burst the lights of the eye's baptism and thus the Holy Spirit's anointment which is within, a light magnificent and true without any lie, will shine.

They opened their hearts

When God's truth was revealed to them regarding the birth of the Messiah they were not only satisfied by the inspiration, but endured the troubles of the journey. The enlightenment of encountering Christ had shone in their hearts and immediately they got up and carried the cross behind Him denying themselves and all the desires and lusts of the world. The hearts of the wise men were opened and were filled with love and joy.

Love and joy ease the suffering in the path of salvation. They did not look at their honour but focused their sight towards Jerusalem. They took no heed to the troubles but desired with joy to see the new born. They did not fall in the way but patiently persevered until they saw the new born who has changed history.

They opened their treasures

When they encountered the Word incarnate, they expressed their love by their offerings and their reverence by kneeling and bowing.

They offered Him gold because the Spirit declared to them that He is the king of the Jews. The Lord ruled over the wood of the cross and the lives of all those who wish to rule with Him cling with the life of the crucified. If we are patient we will rule with Him in the glory of His good Father. The youth who refuse bodily desires and control their instincts will rule with the Lord who spoke the words of a free king: "For the ruler of this world is coming, and he has nothing in Me" (John 14:30).

They offered Him frankincense symbolising His chief priesthood. The Lord took His priesthood with assertion from the Lord "The Lord has sworn and will not relent, You are a priest forever according to the order of Melchizedek" (Psalms 110:4).

The priesthood of Levites in the Old Testament ended with time but we have a living high priest forever interceding for us (Hebrews 7:25). Every high priest in the Old Testament offered a sacrifice for his own sins first before he offered sacrifices for the iniquities of the people. Our great high priest was not in need of offering a sacrifice for Himself because He is holy and righteous. The anointing with the Holy Spirit made Jesus' priesthood overflow to all the members of His blessed body and descends upon every believer to purify and consecrate them for the glory of the Father just like the precious oil upon the head, running down on the beard, the beard of Aaron, running down on the edge of his garments (Psalm 133).

They offered Him myrrh. This symbolises the fact that He would be offered as a sacrifice like a lamb lead to the slaughter and like a sheep roasted over bitter herbs on the eve of the Passover. Jesus through the sacrifice on the cross has completed all the suffering for the salvation of humanity. As for us, our suffering has become with Him and for Him. We have been granted unity in the glory "I now rejoice in my sufferings for you, and fill up in my flesh what is lacking in the afflictions of Christ, for the sake of His body, which is the church" (Colossians 1:24).

We are kings with the grace that controls all our instincts. We are priests by offering ourselves as spiritual bread and a sacrifice of continuous praise. We are rich by the various sufferings we pass through so that we are witnesses for the sake of truth, which was declared to us in Jesus Christ.

Chapter 4

He was Placed for the Fall and Rise of Many

Jesus' parents entered with baby Jesus to the temple to do for Him according to the custom of the law. Simeon the elder stood and prophesised about the child saying "Behold, this Child is destined for the fall and rising of many in Israel, and for a sign which will be spoken against (yes, a sword will pierce through your own soul also), that the thoughts of many hearts may be revealed" (Luke 2:34-35).

The light of nativity has shone on the poor, the meek and the kind and tender hearted who resemble lambs and on all those who lived with hope but were in darkness. The light of the nativity guided their feet into the way of peace (Luke 1:79).

These are God's wondrous intentions that He chose the foolishness of the world to put to shame the wisdom of the wise and chose the meek and weak to put to shame those who are proud of their knowledge, who elevate themselves because of their positions and exalt themselves above the sinner and the poor.

Two types of humanity

When Jesus was born, humanity became divided in two. A meek type, which is spiritual and is pleased by the Lord's salvation and praises the new born in the manger and does not dismiss the One living in the house of Joseph the carpenter. It is not offended by the cross because the spiritual eye reveals to them that even though He was in a manger, He was still the King of Glory who sits upon the heavenly throne ruling over the hearts of the humble. The newborn of Bethlehem started poor wrapped in torn cloths but to the unpretentious and enlightened, He is the giver of life and only He is worthy of honour and praise.

The wise men offered gold because the truth revealed to their eyes His rein and glory. They offered Him frankincense because their spiritual vision illustrated to them his chief priesthood and because He is Holy, He separated from the sinners and became above the heavens. They offered Him myrrh because their spiritual experience revealed to them the depth of His suffering that He planned to taste for the sake of sinners, those who have strayed and those who are lost.

As for Herod, he queried the wise men about the newborn's location in order to kill Him. Ananias, Caiaphas and the Scribes knew the law by heart, yet their hearts were filled with spitefulness, lies, trickery and so felt threatened and could not bear to see the truth but insisted on resisting and clashing with it.

And so from generation to generation, the words of Simeon the elder about Christ will remain as the measure that reveals the authenticity of the spiritual encounter in a person's life. It remains as the measure as to how much they enjoy the truth and the love of witnessing His joy through the free gift of salvation and gift of peace which is given to the saints and to the meek.

Christ came to destroy the arrogant and the wicked. Yet the meek, the humble, the sinner and those who await salvation, the Lord came for their acceptance in order to fulfil Isaiah's prophecy in the Old Testament that every valley shall be exalted and every mountain and hill brought low; The glory of the Lord shall be revealed, And all flesh shall see it together.

A sword will pierce

It would seem somewhat contrary that Simeon the elder would talk about a sword piercing the heart of the Virgin Mary while she is approaching the temple and with her the One whom the angels exalt, proclaiming to the world with great joy when they sang their heavenly song "Glory to God in the highest, And on earth peace". However, this seemingly contradiction soon escapes our mind when we realise that a requirement of real faith is suffering and as the level of faith rises so will the suffering increase in severity and depth. If Philosophers agree that suffering is a measure of a person's humanity and that as man progresses in civility so will his experience in suffering increase, for Christianity considers suffering a necessity for true spiritual encounter.

The Virgin Mary as the highest example for humanity rose in spiritual experience to the extent that she accepted to bear without the seed of man and risked getting stoned according to the Law of Moses. She was the one that Simeon prophesied about that a sword will pierce her heart that the thoughts of many hearts may be revealed.

The prophecy was fulfilled when the Virgin bowed at the feet of the crucified Christ and said "The world rejoices at the acceptance of salvation, but my heart burns when I look at your crucifixion which you endured for the sake of all; O my Son and my God".

And now

We need to examine ourselves and assess our spiritual life in light of these words. Of which kind are we? Where do we stand from the newborn of the manger? Are we prepared for suffering that crushes the heart if we willingly join the Virgin in her joy by the birth of the Saviour and magnify her Son with Simeon the elder saying: "A light to bring revelation to the Gentiles, And the glory of Your people Israel"

Chapter 5

Peace on Earth

One of the prominent names that Isaiah prophesied about the Lord Jesus is that He would be called the Prince of Peace. Isaiah says "For unto us a Child is born, Unto us a Son is given; And the government will be upon His shoulder. And His name will be called Wonderful, Counselor, Mighty God, Everlasting Father, Prince of Peace" (Isaiah 9:6).

Regardless of the different views in the Old Testament about the Messiah, they all agree that it is clear that He is the King of Peace.

Only He is able to achieve for humanity its desired dream and its biggest wish; to remove fear from people and uproot dominance, misuse and lack of trust – all of which proof the lack of peace and safety of the mind.

Peace between nations is an important matter for which the church prays for during the litanies and the ritual and liturgical prayers. The church asks for the governors that God may provide them peaceful days; the church also prays that the Lord delivers us from war, anguish, inflation, pestilence and to rescue man and beast.

The church blesses every humanitarian effort that acts for the sake of reconciling nations and resolving altercations and supporting strong foundations for peace built on justice between people in their different locations and environments.

However, Christian peace is not just about ending war, tribulations and altercations. In its depths it is a model of heavenly life on earth and it is a fruit of the Holy Spirit, which the Holy Bible expressed saying "for the kingdom of God is not eating and drinking, but righteousness and peace and joy in the Holy Spirit" (Romans 14:17).

Let us contemplate on this Godly peace that came for us through the person of the newborn of Bethlehem.

Righteousness and peace have kissed

The beautiful psalmist of Israel sang in his psalm about the Messiah and His wondrous salvation saying "I will hear what God the Lord will speak, For He will speak peace To His people and to His saints; But let them not turn back to folly. Surely His salvation is near to those who fear Him, That glory may dwell in our land. Mercy and truth have met together; Righteousness and peace have kissed. Truth shall spring out of the earth, And righteousness shall look down from heaven. Yes, the Lord will give what is good; And our land will yield its increase. Righteousness will go before Him, And shall make His footsteps our pathway" (Psalm 85:8-13).

The church, which is guided by the Holy Spirit, has put this psalm in the sixth hour in which it remembers the crucifixion of Christ. This is through which we gained salvation and in it truth and mercy converged and righteousness and peace have kissed.

Christ through His incarnation, birth, crucifixion and death by the flesh has fulfilled the divine justice and gave us His personal righteousness in order for us to be reconciled with God and without fault "For He made Him who knew no sin to be sin for us, that we might become the righteousness of God in Him" (2 Corinthians 5:21).

The fruit of this righteousness is true peace that dominates the life of the children of God for which our teacher Paul says "Therefore, having been justified by faith, we have peace with God through our Lord Jesus Christ" (Romans 5:1).

Therefore, the relationship between righteousness and peace is clarified. Christ to whom is due glory justifies us with His grace and grants us peace by His righteousness and the strong bond between those two graces that are inseparable is what is expressed in the psalm "Righteousness and peace have kissed" (Psalm 85:10).

One of the problems of our youth is that they seek peace without focusing on a life of righteousness, piety, obedience and treading in accordance with the commandments of the Lord. The apostle Paul says that Melchizedek who symbolized Christ, was first, the King of Righteousness then the King of Salem, that is the King of Peace (Hebrews 7:2).

Void is any attempt to seek inner peace if Christ, the King of Righteousness, does not rule over the heart first. It is impossible for the person to enjoy real peace before they submit to the One, the Saviour, for their heart to be ruled over.

The Apostolic church lived this life where the faithful sold everything to obtain the precious jewel of high price. As the faith which they obtained by choice ruled over their lives, they lived in peace that stood in the face of Nero's persecution and gave the martyrs power to overcome fierce lions and dangerous beasts. This peace is comparable, if not greater, than that of Paul's while imprisoned in Philippi, whose heart was filled with the Holy Spirit and joy, that he spent the whole night praying, singing and praising with Silas (Acts 16:25). The Book of Acts says, "Then the churches throughout all Judea, Galilee, and Samaria had peace and were edified. And walking in the fear of the Lord and in the comfort of the Holy Spirit, they were multiplied" (Acts 9:31).

This peace was also sung of by the chorus of Angels the day of the birth of the Saviour in Bethlehem.

The Lord granted peace to his saintly disciples saying, "Peace I leave with you, My peace I give to you; not as the world gives do I give to you" (John 14:27). Peace that exceeds every mind that protects our hearts, minds in Jesus Christ.

Unity in the bond of peace

If the Messiah's peace is not granted except through truth and righteousness then His peace is not given except when there is unity of the spirit and of the heart. The Lord Jesus blessed those who make peace, for He called them children of God.

Hundreds of years before the arrival of the Messiah, Isaiah the prophet praised the feet of those who bring good news and proclaim peace and salvation (Isaiah 52:7).

The earth, which enjoys this peace, is God's church. This holy island, around which the furious waves of the world clash, is attired by garments of peace by grace. The prophet David talks about her saying "Praise the Lord, O Jerusalem! Praise your God, O Zion! For He has strengthened the bars of your gates; He has blessed your children within you" (Psalms 147:12) and whenever the apostle Paul spoke about peace, he defined it in the realm of spiritual unity where he says "For God is not the author of confusion but of peace, as in all the churches of the saints" (1 Corinthians 14:33). He also says "And let the peace of God rule in your hearts, to which also you were called in one body; and be thankful" (Colossians 3:15). "with all lowliness and gentleness, with longsuffering, bearing with one another in love, endeavoring to keep the unity of the Spirit in the bond of peace" (Ephesians 4:2-3). He returns to repeat this commandment to the church in Corinth by saying "Be of good comfort, be of one mind, live in peace; and the God of love and peace will be with you" (2 Corinthians 13:11).

Do not expect that everyone will accept the peace of the Lord. There are those who are attached to the world and reject righteousness. The apostle Paul spoke about those people "And the way of peace they have not known" (Romans 3:17). And the Lord, to whom is due glory, spoke about them to His pure apostles saying "And if a son of peace is there, your peace will rest on it; if not, it will return to you" (Luke 10:6).

"There is no peace," says the Lord, "for the wicked."

Miserable is the person who gasps for materialism, money, luxury, pleasure, knowledge and desires and forgets that God's peace, the real peace, is in the heart and it is the only solution to loneliness and emptiness.

Even though Christ's birth has achieved peace on earth, the earth of those hearts that live in righteousness and justice, those that experience unity of the heart and love, patiently await and expect peace. This complete peace of which the Apostle John saw in the new heaven and the new earth when he heard a loud voice from heaven saying "Behold, the tabernacle of God is with men, and He will dwell with them, and they shall be His people. God Himself will be with them and be their God. And God will wipe away every tear from their eyes; there shall be no more death, nor sorrow, nor crying. There shall be no more pain, for the former things have passed away. Then He who sat on the throne said, "Behold, I make all things new"" (Revelation 21:3-5).

My Lord Jesus Christ, my good saviour who was born in Bethlehem, the King of righteousness and peace, give us your peace and let your peace rule over our hearts; our churches, our land and beloved country. Grant us the joy of witnessing to the heavenly Jerusalem the city full of peace, the city of joy wherein the godly wedding is. Grant us to praise joyfully with the chorus of angels your glorified birth.

"Glory to God in the highest, And on earth peace, goodwill toward men"

Chapter 6

Why the Word was Incarnate

Saint Athanasius the Apostolic says "when talking
about our Saviour's incarnation it is imperative that we
talk about the origin of man. God created mankind to
be in a perfect state, but man despised and rejected
contemplation in God, and invented and chose for
themselves wickedness, therefore, they deserved
judgment of death, which they were warned of
beforehand. Their nature has become saturated with
sin...they could no longer rise even from sins that are
against nature". Just as what Saint Paul said "For this
reason God gave them up to vile passions. For even their
women exchanged the natural use for what is against
nature. Likewise also the men, leaving the natural use
of the woman, burned in their lust for one another, men
with men committing what is shameful, and receiving
in themselves the penalty of their error which was due"
(Romans 1:26,27). It is then inappropriate for such a
creation that was created intelligent and one that was in
communion with the Word to be left for desolation and
return to non-existence through corruption. What does
not conform to God's goodness is lead to destruction;
hence the devil lured humanity and creation. Thus it was
shameful and inappropriate that God's work in humanity
be blotted out be it because of their negligence or
because they were lured by the devil. How can God
while He is all good bear to see corruption overshadow
humanity and death thrust its nails in them.

What then is the point of creating them from the

beginning? They would have been better off if they were not created than to be created, neglected and destroyed. Therefore, it became imperative that man would not be left to the current state of corruption, because this would be considered inappropriate and not in accordance with God's goodness.

Incarnation and renewal of the creation

What is the use of creating man in the image of God from the beginning? It would have been better if he was created in the image of beasts that do not speak than to be created with intelligence and speech and to then live like beasts. What could God possibly do? Only to renew this creation, which was in the image of God so that humanity can once again know Him. However, how could this be achieved unless God's image Himself was present – our Lord Jesus Christ? This would have been impossible to fulfill through humanity because we are only created in the image of God, as such, the Word of God Himself, who is the image of the Father, came in order to renew humanity's creation in the form of this image. This would not be possible without the destruction of death and corruption; therefore, it was natural for the Word to take on a body capable of dying so that once He has completely destroyed death in it, it would be possible to renew humanity that was created in its image.

Repentance was insufficient

Would God ask humanity to repent over their iniquities? This would seem appropriate for God, for since they inherited corruption because of iniquity, they are granted incorruption as a result of repentance.

Firstly, repentance was not capable of fulfilling the demands of God the just. God had said that the punishment of sin was death thus God cannot go back on His word, he cannot be dishonest.

Second of all, it would fall short of changing man's nature because as it is, it stands as an obstruction between man and the commitment of another sin. The corruption that occurred was not external to the body, but attached to it, thus it was a requirement that life be attached to it in place of corruption, such then that as death took over the body, so would life.

If death were outside the body it would have been appropriate for life to be externally attached to it. However, death became mingled with the body and ruled over it as if it was united with it and therefore, it was a requirement for life to be mixed with the body too; so that once the body wore life instead of death it would detach corruption from it. It was therefore very reasonable that the saviour took on a body so that once the body united with life, it would no longer remain in death as it was before, but rise to life. Therefore, Christ took on a body in order to be able to encounter death in the body and destroy it. How then would it have been possible to establish that the Lord is life unless He revived what was dead?

Incarnation was for salvation and defeating death

When God saw that every human was under the bondage of death, He had mercy on us and compassion for our weakness and pitied our corruption. He could not bear to see death gain control and for creation to perish. He took for Himself a body matching ours, resembling us in everything except for sin. Everyone was under the rule of corruption and death, so He offered His body on behalf of all in order to nullify the Law that ruled with the destruction of humanity. He restored humanity to incorruption and protected us from death by His body and the grace of His resurrection, which rescued us from death.

He took for Himself a body capable of dying so that He would be able to die on behalf of all and free all from the Law of corruption by the grace of resurrection from death.

To enable the offering of a sacrifice on behalf of others, the Word took a matching body as the Apostle Paul said "the children have partaken of flesh and blood, He Himself likewise shared in the same, that through death He might destroy him who had the power of death, that is, the devil, and release those who through fear of death were all their lifetime subject to bondage" (Hebrews 2:14-15). By the sacrifice of His body, He put a stop to the death sentence which reigned over us and set for us a new beginning and granted us a life with the hope of resurrection.

Was incarnate to guide us to the knowledge of God

What is the point of creation if it does not know its creator or how is it possible for it to be intelligent without knowing the Word of God who brought them into existence? Humans in their error and rebellion were negligent of the grace given to them and left God. Their souls were darkened, not only because they left God, but by inventing idols and heeding the arts of magic and worshiping the devil.

When the Word saw that humans focused their thoughts in matters relating to the body, He descended to the level of their thought and took the form of a body. Since the Lord is good and also looks after His people, He descended to the level of His people, as the Apostle Paul said "For since, in the wisdom of God, the world through wisdom did not know God, it pleased God through the foolishness of the message preached to save those who believe" (1 Corinthians 1:21). He saw that humanity rejected orientation to God and their sight fell short where they searched for gods in the world, inventing for themselves gods from humans who are corrupted. The Word of God took upon Himself a body and walked among people in order to transfer humanity to Himself and focus their senses on Him. Therefore humans look to Him as a person and yet His works proving that He is not just simply human, but God and the Word of God and His wisdom.

Incarnation does not limit God

Let no one imagine that God became limited or that there was a place that was void of His presence because He appeared in a body. Let us not think that the world was denied of His care or management of the universe as long as He was in the body. What is worth pondering is that even though He is the Word and that no place can accommodate Him for He fills every place, yet while He was revealed to all creation He was different from all creation in His essence. While He was in the flesh He continued giving life to the whole universe at the same time without opposition. The sun that we see in the sky, which He created, is not defiled by touching anything from the earth and is not diminished by the earth's darkness, rather it lights it up and purifies it. Such then is the all Holy, the Word of God the creator of the sun. He is the Lord and is not defiled simply by appearing in the flesh, on the contrary, because he cannot be defiled, He revived the body and purified it too.

Chapter 7

Blessed My Nature in Yourself

"O You, the Being throughout all times, have come to us on earth. You have come into the womb of the Virgin. You, the infinite, being God, did not consider equality with God a thing to be grasped, but emptied Yourself and took the form of a servant, and blessed my nature in Yourself, and fulfilled Your Law on my behalf. You have shown me the rising up from my fall. You have given release to those who were bound in Hades. You have lifted the curse of the Law. You have abolished sin in the flesh." Gregorian Liturgy

Yes, you blessed my nature in Yourself. You accepted to unite with this nature, which was cursed by death and resembled us in everything except for sin.

With Your incarnation, man became greater than angles. By becoming man, we enter the Holies with a glorified body. By uniting with the flesh You granted us the Church's sacraments

With Your incarnation, man became greater than angles

The one who looks at the early chapters of Genesis will see that man was created in the image of God and that he was a creature invited to converse directly with God.

When sin entered man by the envy of the devil, it tore the unity between man and God and man fell and descended to the earth, which was cursed because of him, and the judgment was "Till you return to the ground, For out of it you were taken; For dust you are, And to dust you shall return…you shall surely die" (Genesis 2:17, 3:19).

Christ's incarnation and His unity with human nature did not only return man to his original status, which the Bible talks about in "What is man that You are mindful of him, And the son of man that You visit him? For You have made him a little lower than the angels, And You have crowned him with glory and honor" (Psalms 8:4-5), but Christ lifted man to a level where he became higher than an angel.

• Can an angel see the body and blood of Christ on the altar?

• Can an angel partake of these Godly sacraments?

• Can an angel become an altar for the Holy Spirit?

For this reason, St Paul the Apostle of the gentiles, expressed in his saying "For it was fitting for Him, for whom are all things and by whom are all things, in bringing many sons to glory, to make the captain of their salvation perfect through sufferings. For both He who sanctifies and those who are being sanctified are all of one, for which reason He is not ashamed to call them brethren, saying: "I will declare Your name to My brethren; In the midst of the assembly I will sing praise to You"" (Hebrews 2:10-12). And in the same letter he says "Inasmuch then as the children have partaken of flesh and blood, He Himself likewise shared in the same, that through death He might destroy him who had the power of death, that is, the devil" (Hebrews 2:14), "Therefore, in all things He had to be made like His brethren, that He might be a merciful and faithful High Priest in things pertaining to God, to make propitiation for the sins of the people" (Hebrews 2:17).

For humanity through Jesus Christ was given a status greater than the heavenly hosts. The church ranks the Virgin Mary higher and more noble than the Cherubim and the Seraphim and the four incorporeal creatures around the throne of God and refers to her as the second heaven.

Through the incarnation we enter the Holies in a glorified body

The book of Hebrews says "where the forerunner has entered for us, even Jesus, having become High Priest forever according to the order of Melchizedek" (Hebrews 6:20), he continues to say "Therefore, brethren, having boldness to enter the Holiest by the blood of Jesus, by a new and living way which He consecrated for us, through the veil, that is, His flesh, and having a High Priest over the house of God, let us draw near with a true heart in full assurance of faith, having our hearts sprinkled from an evil conscience and our bodies washed with pure water. Let us hold fast the confession of our hope without wavering, for He who promised is faithful" (Hebrews 10:19-23).

What is clear from these verses is that Christ our God through His incarnation and death in the flesh on the cross has opened the true Holy of Holies, which was shut in the face of man because of sin. Christ sacrificed His body for our assurance of entering the Holies, however, we will not enter with our earthly bodies, but our bodies must change and become like those of angels in the image of His glorified body as the Bible says "that flesh and blood cannot inherit the kingdom of God" (1 Corinthians 15:50).

The Bible tells us that we will all change at the sound of the last trumpet because this corruption must wear incorruption and this mortal must put on immortality. Therefore, we who have the first fruits of the spirit mourn within ourselves expecting adoption in place of our bodies when we, along with all of creation are saved from corruption to the freedom of the children of God.

It is a major responsibility on the believer to respect the body, which will receive the glory of transfiguration and enter the Holies itself.

1) We must respect our bodies and not defile it because the body was not created for fornication, but honour,

and whoever defiles the temple of God, God will destroy him.

2) We must respect our bodies, as such, we must not disrespect it by using adornment and beautifications that turn it into a spectacle show to intrigue and stumble others. Cleanliness, grooming and fitness are important, however, finery takes the body away from its origin and mission.

3) We must respect other's bodies and honour it, as such, we must not touch it unless with complete purity and must not look at it inquisitively lest we be cursed like Ham and Canaan.

4) We must also assist in any way we can in helping organisations that are concerned with the growth of man and his safety, such as UNESCO, World Health Organization, Human Rights organizations, International Justice Court, Women Rights organizations, children, disabled, seniors and every organization that fights slavery, racism and abuse to humans wherever they may be.

5) We can earnestly seek with spiritual zeal and perseverance that our Lord God saves the souls of many and fill people's lives with love, joy, peace and salvation, because this Godly light is what will dawn in the second coming and swallow every corruption in our bodies, which will be for the resurrection of life and not for the resurrection of judgment.

Chapter 8

The Word Was Incarnate

If a noble visited a poor person, entered their home and sat with them, it would be considered a great honour for that poor person. How then loving and compassionate would this noble person have been if previously he had been insulted by the poor man yet still visited him.

We are now faced with a situation that exceeds the above situation in terms of importance and respect. Adam sinned against God and disobeyed His commandment, for which death was the punishment. The apostle Paul says "Therefore, just as through one man sin entered the world, and death through sin, and thus death spread to all men, because all sinned" (Romans 5:12).

The earth was cursed, as it is written in Genesis 3, "In the sweat of your face you shall eat bread till you return to the ground, for out of it you were taken; for dust you are, and to dust you shall return." Thus man became grieved.

God in the Old Testament gave his people the law and commandments and sent them prophets and spoke with His chosen ones. He spoke with them; once in the form of three angels, once in the form of an Angel, and once as a flame of fire in the midst of a bush. "God, who at various times and in various ways spoke in time past to the fathers by the prophets, has in these last days spoken to us by His Son, whom He has appointed heir of all things, through whom also He made the worlds" (Hebrews 1:1-2).

In the New Testament, there was no new law given. He provided Himself fully as a human like us, resembling us in everything except for sin only.

In Monday's Theotokia in the church's praises, the church teaches us saying:

• "While Adam was sad, God was pleased to return him back to his leadership. He shone in the flesh, taken from the Virgin, without the seed of man in order to save us."

• Jesus Christ the Word became flesh and made His dwelling among us. We have seen His glory, the glory as of the one and only Son, who came from the Father, full of grace and truth, who was pleased to save us: shone in the flesh.

• Who has always been, came and will come again, Jesus Christ the Word became flesh without blemish became fully human without mixing or alteration or separation in any way after unification, but a single nature, hypostasis, a single person, God the Word shone in the flesh.

• Hail to Bethlehem, the city of the prophets, where Christ the Second Adam was born. In order to bring Adam, the first man, made of dust, back to paradise. And to absolve the decree of death saying "Adam you are from dust, and to dust you shall return. For in the place where sin has abounded, the grace of Christ has abounded more.

• All the spirits rejoiced with the angels praising Christ the king proclaiming and saying, glory to God in the highest, peace on earth and good will to all men. He demolished the barrier, ended the animosity and tore the deed of slavery, which was for Adam and Eve and made them free. He who was born for us in the city of David according to the saying of the angel, Jesus our saviour, shone in the flesh.

• God is light out of light and dwells in light. His angels are spiritual bodies praising Him. The light has shone on Mary and Elizabeth gave birth to the forerunner. The Holy Spirit woke David and said: Get up and sing, because the light has shone, so David the prophet and psalmist got up took his spiritual psaltery and went to the church, the house of angels and praised and sang to the Holy Trinity saying, in your light O Lord we see light, let your mercy come to those who know you. You are the true light that gives light to everyone coming to this world. You came to earth through your love for mankind and all the creation rejoiced, you saved Adam from temptation and delivered Eve from the pangs of death. You gave us the spirit of sonship, we praise you and bless you with your angels: He shone in the flesh from the Virgin without the seed of man and saved us.

We contemplate on these glorious theological truths for the purpose of learning God's objectives and the effect of the Incarnation on man, church and all matter.

God's Objective For The Incarnation:

The Church in its praises tells us 'rejoice O mankind, because God so loved the world that He sent His beloved Son on behalf of those who believe in Him in order to have eternal life. Through His compassion He came down and sent us His almighty Son and shone in the flesh.'

The Incarnation is profoundly tied with the heavenly Father's love. Paul the apostle proclaimed to us the extreme thirst that filled the Father's heart with love that He sent His only beloved Son to become man in order to redeem and save Adam and his children. In Paul's message to the Ephesians he says "having made known to us the mystery of His will, according to His good pleasure which He purposed in Himself, that in the dispensation of the fullness of the times He might gather together in one all things in Christ, both which are in heaven and which are on earth—in Him". Saint Paul goes on to clarify that this will was from before the ages by saying "just as He chose us in Him before the foundation of the world, that we should be holy and without blame before Him in love, having predestined us to adoption as sons by Jesus Christ to Himself, according to the good pleasure of His will" (Ephesians 1:4-6).

How glorious is this will that was filled with love! This, which has made some church fathers say that the world was not created for any reason other than to become a church. The Father's objective of the Son's Incarnation was not confined by salvation for Adam and his children, but His love extended to involve man in a godly life, life of fellowship with the Holy Trinity with unprecedented riches.

God's delight is in mankind; God's love for humanity exceeds any imagination and the Incarnation of God's Son by becoming human is the biggest proof of God's love for us. It is the strongest evidence of God's holy and everlasting providence for the sake of proclaiming His love for mankind, who was created in God's image.

If the cross reveals to us the great love of our Lord Jesus Christ, then how much more does the Incarnation proclaim this tremendous love, which fills the heart of our heavenly Father who accepted for His Son to be Incarnate through the womb of the virgin Mary.

Does not then God's deep love demand our closeness and make us approach Him with gratefulness and offer praise and our life as a sacrifice, devoting our will and love to His blessed person?!

Let our eyes be fixed on Nazareth where the humble Virgin representing humanity received the news of salvation. Let our eyes be fixed towards heaven where the love of God the Father descended, shining over humanity who were sitting in darkness and the shadow of death. Let us faithfully seek to unite with God as He did with us, who gave us what is His and took what is ours. This Godly descend from heaven warrants a natural response from us through the devotion of the heart to the heavenly Father. It warrants the directing of all of the human's strength, mind and feelings towards Him.

This Godly Incarnation reveals something about God's nature. Though He descended for us, it does not mean that He is no longer omnipotent and though He later ascended does not render Him far away from us.

Christians believe that God's Incarnation, in its holy essence, did not occur as an alteration in time. Christians are aware that God is not going to change if He becomes incarnate. The one who believes that God created man from dust in a specific time and in a confined place will also believe that God's Incarnation in a specific era and in a confined place does not make Him limited nor will it cause alteration, because God is capable of everything and nothing is impossible for Him. 'With men this is impossible, but with God all things are possible'.

"God came from you O blessed and perfect one to save the world, which He had created according to His love and mercy. We praise Him and exalt Him above all, O You the good lover of mankind, have mercy on us according to your great mercy".

Incarnation and Man

Humanity fell in the Garden of Eden and all materialistic creation was contaminated when our father Adam and our mother Eve fell in disobedience. While some non-Christians see that repentance is sufficient to restore Adam to his original state, Saint Athanasius the Apostle saw that "repentance is incapable of satisfying the requirements of God the Just, because if man remained in the pangs of death, then God would not be truthful. This is in addition to the fact that repentance is incapable of changing a person's nature, because all it does is stand as a barrier between the person, and repeating the sin. Therefore, if what man had committed had not led to corruption, repentance would have been sufficient, however, corruption became Adam's nature and he was denied the grace, which was previously given him. It was now up to God's Word, who created everything from void, to restore grace to Adam".

In this respect, Saint Athanasius the Protector of the Faith says "and the Word saw that the law of humanity's corruption cannot be void except by death, and that it was impossible for the Word to bear death, because He is everlasting and does not fall under the law of death. Thus He took for Himself a body capable of dying even when united with the Trinity and so He was made worthy of dying on behalf of all people. This is exactly what Saint Paul the Apostle said "For as in Adam all die, even so in Christ all shall be made alive" (1 Corinthians

15:22). In another place he says, "Inasmuch then as the children have partaken of flesh and blood, He Himself likewise shared in the same, that through death He might destroy him who had the power of death, that is, the devil, and release those who through fear of death were all their lifetime subject to bondage." (Hebrews 2:14-15).

Death was not external to Adam's body so that life could be provided externally, but death became mixed with the body, it even ruled over it. Therefore, it was required that life would be mixed with the body so that if the body wore life, death would be abolished from it.

Humanity's mind became shifted completely to materialistic matters. The Word was therefore disguised in the flesh so that as a human He would be able to bring humanity to Him and focus their senses onto His person. This is what Saint Paul the Apostle meant when he said "through faith; that you, being rooted and grounded in love, may be able to comprehend with all the saints what is the width and length and depth and height— to know the love of Christ which passes knowledge; that you may be filled with all the fullness of God." (Ephesians 3:18-19).

God through His Incarnation gave man the ability to contain God within him and not to be far from him – which was the case in the Old Testament. Therefore Christ our Lord says in His prayer of intercession "that they all may be one, as You, Father, are in Me, and I in

You; that they also may be one in Us, that the world may believe that You sent Me." (John 17:21).

In the same prayer, He says "I have declared to them Your name, and will declare it, that the love with which You loved Me may be in them, and I in them" (John 17:26).

God, through His Incarnation, restored man to the perfect image, which was His intention.

We now consider the words of Pontius Pilate about Christ when He was being presented for judgement: "Behold the man!" (John 19:5) 'The man' in the sense that this is real humanity; man in his perfect, realistic and practical image, man in his tenderness and decisiveness, in his sweetness and rigour, meekness and strictness, humility and glory, in his external and internal measure, in his spirit and body together.

Since Christ, man has had mediation to God the Father. Christ became the sole intercessor and mediator for humans to be able to enter the holies, to the Father. After Christ, man overcame grief, because Christ bore our grief and assumed our sorrows through His cross. After Christ, man overcame isolation and emptiness, because Christ became everything to man, all satisfaction, comfort and peace.

Man in Christ has overcome death. Christ has trampled with His death the sting of death and bestowed eternal life upon those in the grave.

Man, in Christ, is invited to be god-like as Saint Athanasius the Apostolic said. God took what is ours and gave us what is His. He took our humanity to grant us His glory.

Incarnation And The Church:

If Christ had not become incarnate, the church would not have come to exist. Is not the church His body? The Lord Jesus sent the Holy Spirit the comforter to work in the church after His ascension so that the work He performed while in the flesh would continue.

The Lord Jesus healed the sick and gave the command for baptism and gave His Holy Body and Holy Blood. Thus the church practices His glorified works as spiritual means. As He endured through temptation, the church also completes this endurance in her children who continually witness to the truth throughout the ages and generations.

Our believe in the Incarnation, explains to us the mission of the church and its role in history. The church, through the Incarnation, is not a social institution, or a denomination or an affectionate bond; it is a vessel of faith. It is three measures of flour with the active and effective yeast of salvation. Any understanding of the church purely at the social level or as a church denomination ruins its true meaning that God intended with His Holy Incarnation.

The church is Christ's sacramental body. Every one of its children draws from it their life, being, gifts and mission. Christ does not recognise a group if the truth is not their focal point and spiritual works and salvation their cornerstone regardless of how much they claim to be active and Christian. The church is the pillar and foundation of the truth. If it abandoned the truth in favour of eccentric ways, it resigns its entity and waives its mission. Through the Incarnation, the church witnesses to the truth with the grace of Christ and the work of the Holy Spirit. Therefore the church always asks the Holy Spirit to be burnt into it and its children – "O Good Lord, do not take Your Holy Spirit away from us, this which You sent upon Your holy disciples and honourable apostles at the third hour. Create a pure heart in me, O God and put a new and loyal Spirit within me, do not banish me from Your presence and do not take Your Holy Spirit from me".

Christ founded the church through His Incarnation to be His sacramental body. The Holy Spirit works effectively with His gifts to complete this body through the uniting and fellowship of the faithful community. Once the body has completed its functions, the Lord will bring time to an end because there is a set date for this sole purpose, which is to prepare the sacramental body and complete its members.

The Holy Spirit brings together all members, He unites their persons and combines talents because the church is a community, a collective "We" and not a collection of "I" that exist. The true image of the church was in the upper room where the Holy Spirit was sent on the fiftieth day after the crucifixion. The disciples were gathered in one spirit, in one accord in mind and heart, praying, worshiping and submitting to the will of God. This is the real meaning of church.

The Holy Spirit utilises His gifts to unite the body and complete it, as the Apostle said: "for to one is given the word of wisdom through the Spirit, to another the word of knowledge through the same Spirit, to another faith by the same Spirit, to another gifts of healings by the same Spirit, to another the working of miracles, to another prophecy, to another discerning of spirits, to another different kinds of tongues, to another the interpretation of tongues. But one and the same Spirit works all these things, distributing to each one individually as He wills. For as the body is one and has many members, but all the members of that one body, being many, are one body, so also is Christ. For by one Spirit we were all baptized into one body—whether Jews or Greeks, whether slaves or free—and have all been made to drink into one Spirit. For in fact the body is not one member but many." (1 Corinthians 12:8-14)

Attaining to this perspective, we can thus comprehend the care given to the liturgical prayers by the church in asking for a united heart so that love is rooted in all its members.

Through the liturgy, every member is capable of changing their nature. Those with a hardened heart are transformed through the partaking of the Holy Body and Blood to an enlightened and sensitive member, showing love in harmony enabling them to cohere with others to become a company of saints - which then is truly the church.

How amazing are You O Lord! That You and You alone are capable of making many become one through Your Incarnation. You gathered the scattered, dry and rotten bones and with it, established a living and growing church. You poured over it Your love, and the Holy Spirit the comforter.

How glorified is the church, the bride of Christ! You are a garden enclosed, a spring shut up and a fountain sealed. You are dark but lovely. You have ravished the Father's heart and He saw your beauty through Christ, without fault, as fair as the moon, clear as the sun, awesome as an army with banners.

Incarnation And Matter

The atheist philosopher, Feuerbach, once said "the human is no more than the substance he eats". What he tried to do in this statement is to put an end to principles that voice the spiritual nature of humanity.

The definition of man appeared in the Holy Bible many centuries before Feuerbach. The story of creation pictures man as a hungry being for which God made the world for food. In order for man to increase and rule over the earth, God taught him to eat from it (Genesis 1:29). The likening of the world to a feast appeared numerous times in the Holy Bible, for it is the image of life in it is beginning and end "that you may eat and drink at My table in My kingdom" (Luke 22:30).

The truth of the Incarnation has given matter a new meaning. Matter is no longer defiled nor is the earth corrupt, for Christ has purified the universe with His Incarnation. Christ, through His Incarnation, has sanctified matter. Christ was present in the world not only contributing to its history, but to its very essence as described by a contemporary figure.

The Son of God took the form of a human body forever. The human nature can not be separated from the person of Christ. This is why the church forbade Nestorius the heretic because he separated the divinity from humanity. The church also forbade Eutyches the heretic because he called for the confusion between the human nature and the divine nature in Christ.

Thus it is fitting for us to now understand the use of matter such as bread, wine, oil and water as practicing the sacraments. The cursed earth is what produces the bread and wine that becomes the Body and Blood of the Lord in the Eucharist. As the Virgin prepared her body for the Lord from her blood, so too does created nature and matter produce the bread and wine, which are converted into the Lord's Body and Blood as eternal life for those who partake of it. Matter is no longer defiled or cursed, be it in a human form or in the external realm, because Christ's divinity in His Incarnation and birth has come in contact with matter and His divinity united with His humanity. In the manger the heavenly breath and the earthly breath converged. The humanistic instincts, which had become defiant because of Adam's sin of disobedience, have returned, through unity with the Eucharist to its original state. The sexual instinct is not for pleasure and dominance, but it is a blessed domain for the true Christian to propel towards the other in the scope of love and holy matrimony.

The earthly food is no longer a symbol of disgrace and the fall. The real believer eats of it with a spirit of prayer, asceticism, temperance and gratitude from the hand of God who blessed, sanctified, broke and gave it in the past and till this day He blesses, sanctifies, and gives in His church with His Holy Spirit. The earthly food in itself is no longer for voracity and pleasure, but also for gratitude, bestowal and company of brethren for the Bible says that they were eating the food with joy and a simple heart "breaking bread from house to house, they ate their food with gladness and simplicity of heart, praising God and having favour with all the people" (Acts 2:46-47).

The substance of matter was not changed after the

Incarnation. However, the Incarnation gave it a new meaning and a new look. It gave it a taste of the new earth of which we await the second coming of our faithful Lord.

Ever since the world was enlightened by the light of the Word, we looked at the world through renewed and pure eyes. It is fitting for us to say that God the incarnate has changed the face of this world.

God has changed time when He made the body a temple for the Holy Spirit. Water, oil, bread and wine became realms for unification between God and matter. God's Holy Spirit blows in it to become effective in indescribable sacraments.

Blessed is God the Father who gave His Son to dwell among us as a servant to break free all those besieged by the enslavement of Satan and death.

Blessed is God the Son, the Word who revived us and took our nature to give us His.

Blessed is the Holy Spirit that works in the church of God in every place and throughout the ages to fulfill the purpose of God's Incarnation and complete the church's mission.

Blessed is every invited and chosen believer who has received the most supreme sacraments through grace and who have seen with their eyes God's everlasting intention, which were from before the ages, but were proclaimed to the angels through the church. These matters, which the angels and the prophets from before desired to see, but have not seen them and to hear them, but have not heard them.

As for us, blessed are our eyes because they see and our ears because they hear. May we be worthy to hear and to act according to your Holy Gospels. May we be worthy to fulfill your glorified will and complete, in your church with your Holy Spirit your holy ordinances, which are full of light, peace and salvation.

Chapter 9

The Purpose of the Incarnation accourding to Saint Athanasius the Apostolic

Only the Word's nature is capable of renewing all His creation and to bear all the suffering on behalf of us all and to be a mediator and an intercessor to the Father on behalf of us all.

To nullify the law that sentenced humans to destruction, whereby everyone died by it. Thus to restore humans to non-corruption and revive them from death with His body and the grace of resurrection.

To be able to offer a sacrifice on behalf of our bodies, the Word took a body (He too took flesh and blood in order to destroy Satan who had the power of death). Therefore, by the sacrifice of His Body, He put a stop to the death sentence placed against us.

To show us the heavenly Father, because after man's fall, he deviated to worshiping idols and followed magic and sorcery.

Through His Incarnation, He renewed the creation, which was in the image of God.

Man's thoughts through the fall had shifted to worldly matters, thus the Word appeared in the form of a body to be able to, as a human, transfer humanity over to Him and refocus our senses to His person.

He came to lift off the curse placed over us and by His

death, He became an atonement for all. He abolished the middle wall and as His Body was lifted onto the wood of the cross, he drew all men to Himself.

 To fulfill the many prophecies that fill the holy books about His birth, suffering and death.

 He came in the form of man not just in the shape of one because out of the whole creation, it was man who sinned. He came to save us not to astonish or to influence minds.

 The Word was incarnate and became man in order for us to be become gods. God became man so that man might become god.

(This does not mean that we will be part of His essence or Hypostasis, but we have the ability to share His glorified nature, joy and godly love).

.

www.ingramcontent.com/pod-product-compliance
Lightning Source LLC
Chambersburg PA
CBHW051849040426
42447CB00006B/760